HEINEMANN
BEGIN

GH00888841

MARGARET TARNER

This is Oxford

HEINEMANN

BEGINNER LEVEL

Series Editor: John Milne

The Heinemann Guided Readers provide a choice of enjoyable reading material for learners of English. The Series is published at five levels – Starter, Beginner, Elementary, Intermediate and Upper. At **Beginner Level**, the control of content and language has the following main features:

Information Control
The stories are written in a fluent and pleasing style with straightforward plots and a restricted number of main characters. The cultural background is made explicit through both words and illustrations. Information which is vital to the story is clearly presented and repeated where necessary.

Structure Control
Special care is taken with sentence length. Most sentences contain only one clause, though compound sentences are used occasionally with the clauses joined by the conjunctions 'and', 'but', and 'or'. The use of these compound sentences gives the text balance and rhythm. The use of Past Simple and Past Continuous Tenses is permitted since these are the basic tenses used in narration and students must become familiar with these as they continue to extend and develop their reading ability.

Vocabulary Control
At **Beginner Level** there is a controlled vocabulary of approximately 600 basic words, so that students with a basic knowledge of English will be able to read with understanding and enjoyment. Help is also given in the form of vivid illustrations which are closely related to the text.

For further information on the full selection of Readers at all five levels in the series, please refer to the Heinemann Readers catalogue.

CONTENTS

	Introduction	4
1	History of the City	5
2	History of the University	7
3	The City and the University	13
4	Looking Around Oxford	18
5	Things to See and Do	24
6	Information and Advice	31

INTRODUCTION

Oxford is a city on the River Thames. The city is about 100 km to the west of London. People have lived in Oxford for over a thousand years. Now it is a busy, modern city. Oxford is famous for its university. It is the oldest university in England.

Visitors to Oxford sometimes ask, 'Where is the university?' It is a difficult question to answer. The university has no campus. The university is the collection of all the colleges and their students.

Oxford – a view of the city

Two rivers meet at Oxford. They are the Thames and the Cherwell. The Thames in Oxford is called the Isis. People crossed the water at a shallow place or ford. Oxen pulled carts across the ford too. So the place was called Oxenford or Oxford.

St Frideswide

In the eighth century, a princess lived in Oxford. Her name was Frideswide. A wicked man wanted to marry her. So Frideswide asked for God's help. She left Oxford in a boat and hid on a farm.

St Frideswide's story in the coloured window of Christ Church Cathedral

5

The man tried to follow her. But God made him blind and Frideswide escaped. She founded an important monastery in AD 727 and died in 740. Is this story completely true? We are not sure. But the monastery made Oxford famous.

The Normans

The Normans came to England in 1066. The Norman army defeated the English army. Their leader, William of Normandy, became king of England. The Normans built many castles. King William's friend, Robert d'Oilly, built a castle at Oxford. You can see a small part of it on the Castle Mound.

The Middle Ages (AD 1100-1500)

In 1142, there was a war in England. The Empress Matilda was trapped by King Stephen in Oxford Castle. It was winter and snow covered everything. So Matilda wore a white dress and escaped across the frozen river.

By 1240, Oxford had a strong wall round it. The town had gates to the north, south, east and west. Four roads met in the centre of the city. This central place is called Carfax.

Carfax Tower

2 HISTORY of the UNIVERSITY

The university is not as old as the city. Until 1167, English students went to the University of Paris. But in that year, there was some trouble between England and France. All the English students returned to England. There were good religious teachers, or masters, in Oxford. So the students went there.

The First Students

The students were young and poor. The people of Oxford did not like them. The students lived together for safety.

In 1209, a student killed a woman by mistake. The student ran away. The people of Oxford were very angry. They hanged two of the student's friends. All the other students were afraid. Many of them left the city.

But the Church wanted to help the students. The Church made an agreement with the students and their masters. The agreement was called a Charter. By 1214, the students were back in Oxford. The students and the masters now had a wise man to look after them. He was their Chancellor.

The First Colleges

There was now a University of Oxford. But there were no colleges and very little money. This was a difficult time for the new university. It was saved by a rich man – William of Durham. (say: **Durum**) William died in 1249. He gave the university a large sum of money. The money was used to found the first Oxford college – *University College*.

A few years later, a man was in trouble with the Church. The man's name was John de Balliol. The Church told him to found an Oxford college. *Balliol College* was founded in 1263.

Then, in 1264, Walter de Merton founded a third college. *Merton College* had a hall, a library and a chapel with a big tower. It also had a strong gate! The Masters' rooms were built round a square. The squares are called quadrangles. The quadrangle at Merton – Mob Quad – is the oldest in the university. It is also one of the smallest.

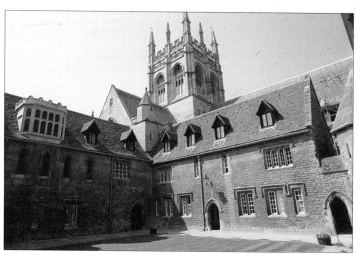

Mob Quad, Merton College

On one side of Mob Quad is the library. Later, other colleges copied Walter de Merton's plan. Most colleges in Oxford have several quads. These quads were built at different times. Even the oldest colleges have some new buildings.

Worcester College, old and new buildings

There are now 36 colleges in Oxford. More than 14 500 people study there.

Women at Oxford

Until 1878, Oxford University was only for men. Women were not clever enough to study. (That is what men said!) Then, in 1873, someone called A.M.A.H. Rogers passed the examination to go to *Worcester College*. But A.M.A.H. Rogers was a woman! She was not allowed to study there. So women decided to have their own colleges. The first women's college, Lady Margaret Hall, was opened in 1879.

By 1893, there were four colleges for women. Until 1974, men and women studied at different colleges. Now all the colleges are co-educational, except one. *St Hilda's* is still only for women.

The first women students – Lady Margaret Hall, 1879

Student Life

The first Oxford students were poor. Later, many of the students were very rich. Some of them did no work at all. Students today have to work very hard. For most students, the final examinations take place after three years.

But students enjoy life too. There are many clubs to join. The largest club is the Oxford Union Society. It holds debates and invites famous people to speak. Mother Teresa and Kermit the Muppet frog, have both spoken at the Oxford Union!

Some Famous People

Many famous people have studied at Oxford. Not all of them got a degree – for example, Dr Samuel Johnson, the poet Shelley, and US President Bill Clinton. But Dr Johnson and President Bill Clinton were given honorary degrees.

Samuel Johnson

Dr John Radcliffe gave a lot of money to the university. He also gave his name to the *Radcliffe Camera*, the *John Radcliffe Hospital* and the *Radcliffe Observatory*. T.E. Lawrence (Lawrence of Arabia) was at *Exeter College*. So was Professor J.R.R. Tolkein. He wrote 'The Lord of the Rings'. Charles Dodgson lived and worked in *Christ Church*. He was the author Lewis Carroll who wrote 'Alice in Wonderland'. The writer, Oscar Wilde, was at *Magdalen College*. (say: **Mawdlin**) T.S. Eliot, the poet, was at Merton.

Dr John Radcliffe

Lewis Carroll

Many famous women studied at Oxford too. Indira Gandhi, Benazir Bhutto and Margaret Thatcher all became politicians. Professor Dorothy Hodgkin won a Nobel Prize for Chemistry in 1964. Aung San Suu Kyi of Burma was given the Nobel Peace Prize in 1991.

Oscar Wilde

Aung San Suu Kyi

Lady Margaret Thatcher

Indira Gandhi

3 THE CITY and the UNIVERSITY

Blood in the Streets!

As time went by, more and more students came to Oxford. The people of Oxford became very unhappy.

Then, on 10th February 1355, something terrible happened. Some students were drinking in an inn (or pub) near Carfax. They did not like the wine. So they threw the pot of drink at the inn-keeper! He shouted for help. Soon everyone nearby was fighting.

Fighting in the streets, 1355

All the students helped their friends. Thousands of people joined in the fight. Then people broke into the students' houses. They destroyed books, food – everything. The fighting went on for three days. Sixty students were killed.

The king was very angry. He made the people of Oxford pay for everything. The university had a new Charter. It was given more power over the city too. For example, the university decided the prices of food and drink. This power lasted for nearly 500 years.

The Civil War

The English Civil War began in 1642. It started because King Charles I disagreed with his Parliament. King Charles moved from London. He made Oxford his capital. The colleges gave their gold and silver to the king. But the people of Oxford supported Parliament and its leader, Oliver Cromwell. Cromwell won the war, but he did not punish the university. England had a king again in 1660 – King Charles II.

The City Grows

In the eighteenth century, the city became richer and richer. More people lived there. There were new roads and a canal in Oxford. The canal workers needed houses. They were built in an area called Jericho. By 1844, Oxford had a railway station. More small houses were built for the railway workers.

The rich tradespeople in the city wanted big new

houses. They built them in North Oxford. From 1877, the university teachers, or dons, were allowed to marry. They built big houses in North Oxford too.

The Car Comes to Oxford

In 1912, William Morris opened a small factory in Cowley, south-east of Oxford. He began to make cars there. There was soon a big factory in Cowley. Cars are still made there. Cowley, and other villages around Oxford, became part of the city.

Cars made a big difference to Oxford. The pollution from the cars damaged the soft stone of the college buildings. The city's roads were crowded with traffic. Now heavy traffic uses the Oxford Ring Road. Visitors park their cars in special places outside the city. They come into Oxford by bus. The stone of the old buildings is now clean. And the city and the university are now working together in an important way. They are building the new *Oxford Science Park* in the north of Oxford. Many people will work there.

Oxford's Other University

In 1992, Oxford Polytechnic became *Oxford Brookes University*. It is in Headington, less than 2 km from the city centre. Oxford Brookes has both full-time and part-time students. They come from all over the world and study many different subjects.

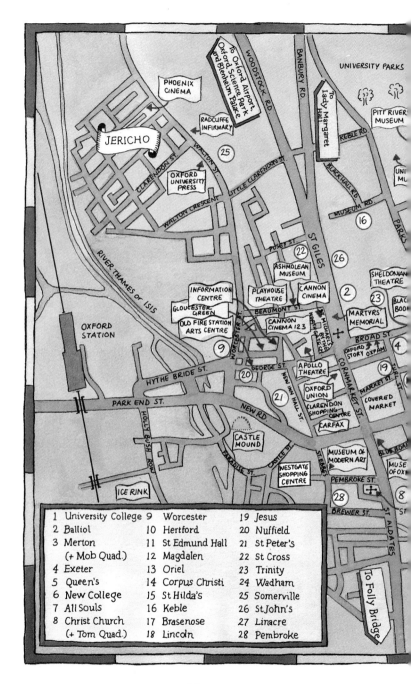

1	University College	9	Worcester	19	Jesus
2	Balliol	10	Hertford	20	Nuffield
3	Merton (+ Mob Quad.)	11	St Edmund Hall	21	St Peter's
4	Exeter	12	Magdalen	22	St Cross
5	Queen's	13	Oriel	23	Trinity
6	New College	14	Corpus Christi	24	Wadham
7	All Souls	15	St Hilda's	25	Somerville
8	Christ Church (+ Tom Quad.)	16	Keble	26	St John's
		17	Brasenose	27	Linacre
		18	Lincoln	28	Pembroke

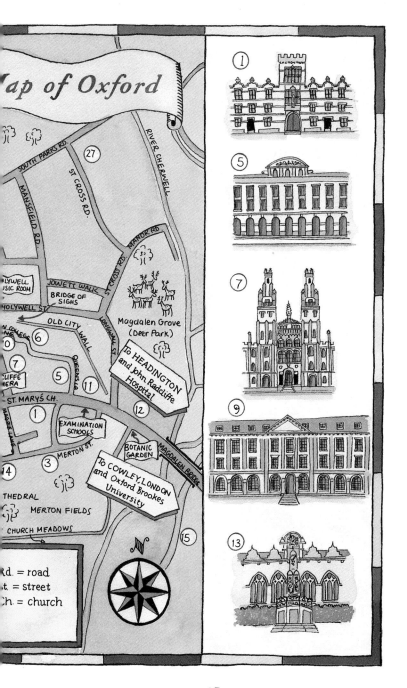

Map of Oxford

SOUTH PARKS RD.
RIVER CHERWELL
27
ST CROSS RD.
MANSFIELD RD.
MANOR RD.
ST CROSS RD.
JOWETT WALK
HOLYWELL
MUSIC ROOM
BRIDGE OF
SIGHS
HOLYWELL ST.
OLD CITY WALL
Magdalen Grove
(Deer Park)
N COLLEGE
ANE
6
To HEADINGTON
and John Radcliffe
Hospital
LONGWALL ST.
QUEENS LA.
7
CLIFFE
ERA
5
11
ST. MARY'S CH.
1
12
EXAMINATION
SCHOOLS
MAGDALEN BRIDGE
14
3
MERTON ST.
BOTANIC
GARDEN
To COWLEY, LONDON
and Oxford Brookes
University
THEDRAL
MERTON FIELDS
CHURCH MEADOWS
15
Rd. = road
t. = street
h. = church

4 LOOKING AROUND OXFORD

The best way to see Oxford is to walk. You can pay a tourist guide to show you the city. You don't like walking? Then you can also see part of the city from a tourist bus!

Or you can look at the city from the water. Go punting on one of Oxford's rivers – the Cherwell. But be careful! Punting isn't easy!

Carfax is a good place to start a walk. First, climb to the top of *Carfax Tower* and look down at the city. Then walk down the High Street.

On the left, is *St Mary's Church*. You can also climb this tower for another good view of the city.

Behind St Mary's is Radcliffe Square. This lovely place is the centre of the university. The round building in the square is the Radcliffe Camera. ('camera' is Latin for room.) It is part of the great *Bodleian Library*. Sir Thomas Bodley began collecting books for the library in 1598. He gave money for new buildings too. So the whole library was named after him.

The Bodleian Library is offered a copy of every book published in Britain. Many of these books are stored under the ground. There are nearly six million books there!

On the right of Radcliffe Square there are two iron gates. Look through them to a beautiful quadrangle and two high towers. This is part of *All Souls College*.

A tourist bus in Broad Street

Punts on the river

A 'gargoyle' carved in stone

The Radcliffe Camera

From the square, walk through a gateway into the Schools Quadrangle and the Bodleian Library. You can visit *Duke Humfrey's Library*. It is the oldest part of the Bodleian. It was first opened in 1488.

Duke Humfrey's Library

Next to the Bodleian is the *Sheldonian Theatre* in Broad Street. It was designed by the famous architect Sir Christopher Wren. Students are given their degrees there. There is a row of stone heads outside the Sheldonian. Who are they? No one knows!

The stone heads outside the Sheldonian Theatre

From the Sheldonian, you can see a pretty little bridge. This bridge goes over a narrow street, New College Lane.

Bridge of Sighs, New College Lane

Go down this street to *New College*. Is this a modern college? No. New College was founded in 1379! New College has an interesting chapel and beautiful gardens. At the end of the gardens, is part of the old city wall.

Magdalen College has beautiful gardens too. It also has a deer park and the most famous tower in Oxford. On 1st May, 'May Day', the college choir sings from the top of the tower. Many people come to listen. Students come by boat to Magdalen Bridge. People stand in the High Street. Everyone must get up very early. The choir sings at 6 am!

Magdalen Tower, Magdalen Bridge

Another very famous college is Christ Church, in St Aldate's. This college had two founders. The first founder was Cardinal Wolsey. The college was founded in 1525 and was called Cardinal College. You can see a statue of Wolsey over the main gate.

Above the statue is Tom Tower. This tower was designed by Sir Christopher Wren. Inside the tower is a huge bell – Great Tom.

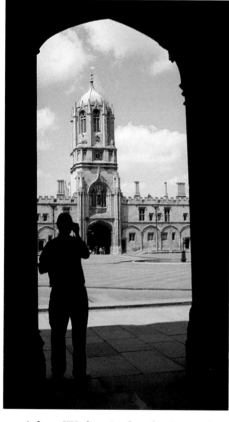

Tom Tower, Christ Church

After Wolsey's death, King Henry VIII took over the college and changed its name to Christ Church.

The chapel at Christ Church is Oxford's cathedral. The cathedral is 300 years older than the college. Do you remember St Frideswide? One of the brightly coloured windows in the cathedral tells her story.

5 THINGS to SEE and DO

Oxford has thousands of visitors every year. They look at the college buildings. They buy things from the city's shops. Oxford is now a modern city with the oldest university in England.

Museums and Art Galleries

The *Ashmolean Museum* in Beaumont Street is named after Elias Ashmole. He gave his treasures to the university at the end of the eighteenth century. The Ashmolean has beautiful and unusual things from all over the world.

Guy Fawkes' lantern

'The Hunt in the Forest' by Paolo Uccello

You can also see beautiful paintings, a jewel made for King Alfred and Guy Fawkes' lantern.

King Alfred's jewel

The *University Museum* is in the centre of Oxford. It was built in the nineteenth century. It is a huge building with a glass roof. You can see dinosaur bones here and a small part of a very strange bird called a dodo.

The University Museum –
a picture of a dodo
and dinosaur bones

There are more strange things to see in the *Pitt Rivers Museum*. It is behind the University Museum. It contains objects from all over the world: weapons, dolls, boats and ornaments.

The *Museum of Modern Art*, in Pembroke Street, has exhibitions of paintings, photographs, films and sculptures.

The *Museum of Oxford*, in St Aldate's, tells us about the city of Oxford and its exciting history.

The *Oxford Story*, in Broad Street, is something completely different. Take a ride and listen to a tape telling you about the university's history! Commentaries are in English and five other languages.

Churches and Memorials

At the north end of Cornmarket is *St Michael's Church*. The tower is the oldest building in Oxford. It is 1000 years old. *Bocardo*, the city's prison, once stood next to St Michael's. The Oxford Martyrs were imprisoned there. These three religious men spoke against the Church in the sixteenth century. They were later burnt to death. They are remembered by the *Martyrs' Memorial* in St Giles'.

Martyrs' Memorial

Parks and Gardens

The *Parks* is a large area of land in North Oxford. You can walk through the Parks to the River Cherwell.

The *University Botanic Garden* is near Magdalen Bridge. Go through the stone arch into this peaceful place. The Botanic Garden has over 8000 kinds of plants.

Christ Church Meadow is a lovely place to walk. There are good views of the city from here.

Shopping

Oxford is a very good place for shopping. There are big stores in *Cornmarket* and *Queen Street*. The *Westgate* is the biggest shopping centre.

University Botanic
Gardens

Covered Market

The Covered Market is behind the High Street. You can buy anything there: delicious food, flowers and interesting clothes. It is a very good place to shop in wet weather! There is another market at Gloucester Green and good shops too.

Little Clarendon Street, off St Giles', has unusual things to buy. *St Clement's* and *Jericho* are other good shopping areas.

Opposite the Sheldonian, in Broad Street, is the famous old bookshop, *Blackwell's*. The first shop used to be very small. It only held four people. Today, many of the shops in Broad Street are part of Blackwell's Bookshop.

The *Oxfam Shop* is also in Broad Street. This was the first shop opened in Britain by the charity, Oxford Committee for Famine Relief. It was opened in 1948.

Food and Drink

There are many good pubs in Oxford. Some popular ones are the *Bear,* the *Eagle and Child* and the *Turf.* What kind of food do you like? French? Chinese? Indian? English? You can find them all in Oxford. You can have a sandwich or an expensive three-course meal.

Plays and Films

The *Playhouse* is the best-known theatre. The *Apollo* shows plays, operas and ballet. The *Old Fire Station Arts Centre* has plays and live music too. The *Pegasus* is Oxford's youth theatre. It holds courses and workshops for young people. Oxford has several cinemas. The *Phoenix Cinema* often shows foreign films. In June, many colleges have plays in their lovely gardens.

Music

There is always music in Oxford. The city has its own orchestra. You can hear classical music in college chapels and the *Holywell Music Room*.

The *Old Fire Station* is great for live music and dancing. It's open every night. The *Jericho Tavern* is good for rock. Many other pubs have live music.

Sport

Races on the River Isis

The Oxford and Cambridge Boat Race takes place in London, on the River Thames. Rowing is popular in

Oxford too. The Bumps' Races are in February and May. The boats race one behind the other. They try to bump the boat ahead and take a higher place. It's very exciting!

Try ice-skating at the Oxford Ice Rink. Or go swimming at the Ferry Pool in Summertown. There are several good sports centres outside the city.

The Countryside Around Oxford

The countryside around Oxford is very beautiful. Woodstock is a pretty town about 12 km from the city. *Blenheim Palace* is there too. Blenheim is the largest private house in England. Look round the house, walk in the grounds. Or take a boat on the lake.

Blenheim Palace, Woodstock

6 INFORMATION and ADVICE

Perhaps you will visit Oxford one day. Will you be a tourist? Or will you be a student? Here is some useful information to help you. Enjoy your stay!

Oxford Information Centre:
The Old School,
Gloucester Green
Tel: (01865) 726871
Phone: *Touristline* for a
recorded message of the
day's events.
Tel: (01865) 244880
Read: *Daily Information* and
This Month in Oxford. (Free
leaflets)

Main Post Office:
St Aldate's
Bus and coach information:
Gloucester Green
Train information:
Oxford Station Travel Centre
Tel: (01865) 722333

Emergency Services:
Ambulance, Fire, Police –
dial 999 (Free).

Heinemann English Language Teaching
A division of Reed Educational and Professional Publishing Limited
Halley Court, Jordan Hill, Oxford OX2 8EJ

OXFORD   MADRID   FLORENCE   ATHENS   PRAGUE
SÃO PAULO   MEXICO CITY   CHICAGO   PORTSMOUTH (NH)
TOKYO   SINGAPORE   KUALA LUMPUR   MELBOURNE
AUCKLAND   JOHANNESBURG   IBADAN   GABORONE

ISBN 0 435 27184 9

Text © Margaret Tarner 1995
Design © Heinemann Publishers (Oxford) Ltd 1995
First published 1995

Acknowledgements
The author and publishers would like to thank the following for permission to
reproduce their photographs and artwork: Ashmolean Museum, Oxford p24
(t/m/b); BMIHT/Rover Group p15; Chris Donohue/The Oxford Photo Library
p29; Mary Evans Picture Library p11 (t/m/b), p12 (t); First students 1879 request-
ed and reproduced with kind permission of the Governing Body of Lady Margaret
Hall p10; The Oxford Story/Heritage Projects p13; The Oxford University
Museum, University of Oxford p25 (l/r); Rex Features p12 (m/bl/br); Thomas
Photos p3, p20 (t); Cartography by Philip's © Reed International Books Ltd. p3.
Commissioned photography by Chris Honeywell p4, p5, p6, p8, p9 (l/r), p19
(t/ml/bl/br), p20 (b), p21, p22, p23, p26, p27 (t/b), p30, p31

Typography by Adrian Hodgkins
Designed by Sue Vaudin
Cover by Tim Richardson and Marketplace Design
Typeset in 12/16pt Goudy
Printed and bound in Malta by Interprint Limited

97   98   99   10   9   8   7   6   5   4   3   2